Published in the United States of America by Cherry Lake Publishing Group
Ann Arbor, Michigan
www.cherrylakepublishing.com

Reading Adviser: Beth Walker Gambro, MS, Ed., Reading Consultant, Yorkville, IL

Photo Credits:
© LuckyStep/Shutterstock, cover (shark), page 23 (top, © Alessandro De Maddalena/Shutterstock cover (seal), page 20 (top), © klyaksun/Shutterstock (graphic on cover and throughout book); © Cassette Bleue/Shutterstock, speech bubbles throughout; © Nazarkru/Shutterstock, yellow bursts throughout; © vitacopS/istockphoto, dark water photo used in background throughout book; © Sergey Uryadnikov/Shutterstock page 3, page 11, page 19 (bottom), page 21 (top); © Martin Prochazkacz/Shutterstock, page 4; © RamonCarretero/istockphoto (top), © VisionDive/Shutterstock (bottom shark), © Save nature and wildlife/Shutterstock (illustration) page 5; © Viacheslav Lopatin/Shutterstock (map), © Gianmarco Cicuzza/Shutterstock, page 6; © USO/istockphoto page 7; © RamonCarretero/istockphoto, page 8; © Grisha Shoolepoff/istockphoto (top), © BELOW_SURFACE/istockphoto (bottom shark), © geckophoto/istockphoto (jaws) page 9; © Ramon Carretero/Shutterstock (top), © Alessandro De Maddalena/Shutterstock, page 10, 12 15 (seal); © okili77/Shutterstock page 12 (map), © ArCaLu/Shutterstock (top), © Valerio Bonaretti/Shutterstock, page 13; © cookyourtrips.com/Shutterstock (both) page 14; © Shane Myers Photography/Shutterstock (shark), page 15; © Piu_Piu/Shutterstock (top), © kavram/Shutterstock, page 16; © Nadezda Murmakova/Shutterstock, page 17; © Mark F Lotterhand/Shutterstock, page 18; © Cathy Withers-Clarke/Shutterstock (top); © Vaclav Sebek/Shutterstock, page 21 (bottom); © Tony Campbell/Shutterstock, page 22 (both); © Black Morion/Shutterstock (top shark), © Bossa Art/Shutterstock (top seal), © Willyam Bradberry/Shutterstock (bottom shark), © Sergey Uryadnikov/Shutterstock (bottom seal), page 23.

Produced for Cherry Lake Publishing by bluedooreducation.com

Copyright © 2026 by Cherry Lake Publishing Group

All rights reserved. No part of this book may be reproduced or utilized in any form or by any means without written permission from the publisher.

Library of Congress Cataloging-in-Publication Data has been filed and is available at catalog.loc.gov.

Printed in the United States of America

Note from Publisher: Websites change regularly, and their future contents are outside of our control. Supervise children when conducting any recommended online searches for extended learning opportunities.

About the Author

Julie K. Lundgren grew up in northern Minnesota near Lake Superior. She delighted in picking berries, finding cool rocks, and trekking in the woods. She still does! Julie's interest in nature science led her to a degree in biology. She adores her family, her sweet cat, and Adventure Days.

Contents

DEADLIEST KILLER 4
I AM A SUPER PREDATOR! 8
FAST AND DELICIOUS 12
GET OUT ALIVE! 18
FIND OUT MORE 24
GLOSSARY 24
INDEX 24

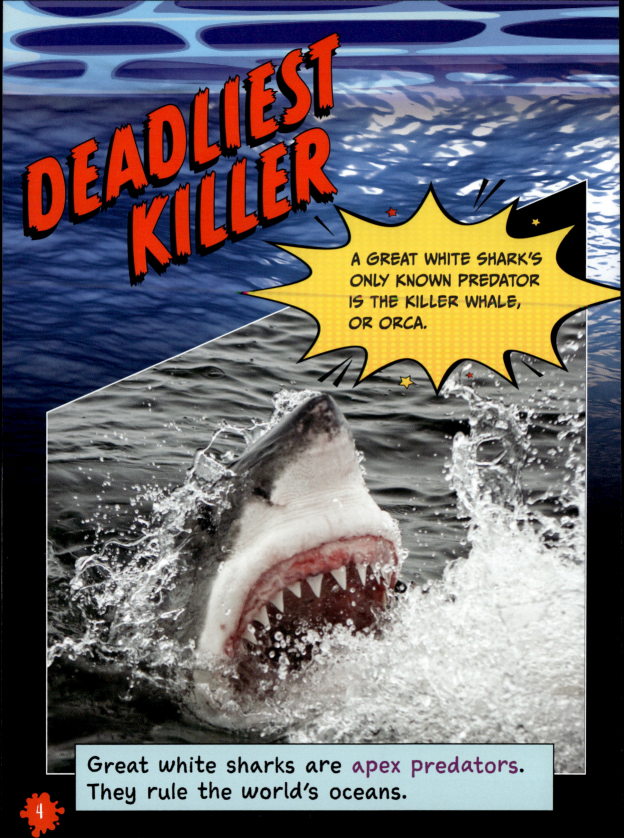

I get my name from my white underbelly.

They grow to 15-20 feet (4.6-6 meters) long. That is about as long as 4 to 5 third-graders laying end to end.

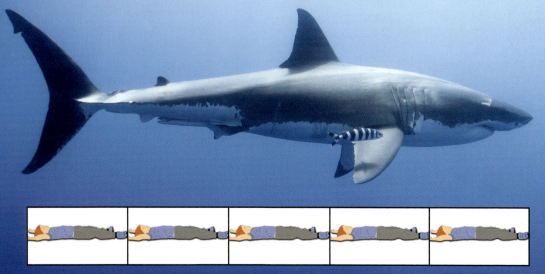

They eat fish, rays, sea turtles, seals, sea lions, and smaller sharks.

GREAT WHITE SHARK MOTHERS SOMETIMES EAT THEIR OWN PUPS!

DORSAL FIN

SHARKS MUST ALWAYS SWIM. THEIR SLEEK AND POWERFUL BODIES HELP DRIVE THIS CONSTANT MOVEMENT. THEY ALSO HAVE A STIFF DORSAL FIN TO KEEP THEM FROM ROLLING AS THEY SWIM.

GREAT WHITES HAVE 300 SHARP TEETH TO RIP APART PREY.

Great white sharks surprise their prey from below.

They race upwards to grab them in one bite.

They often breach the surface of the water.

BREACHING ALLOWS SHARKS TO CAPTURE FAST PREY, LIKE SEALS.

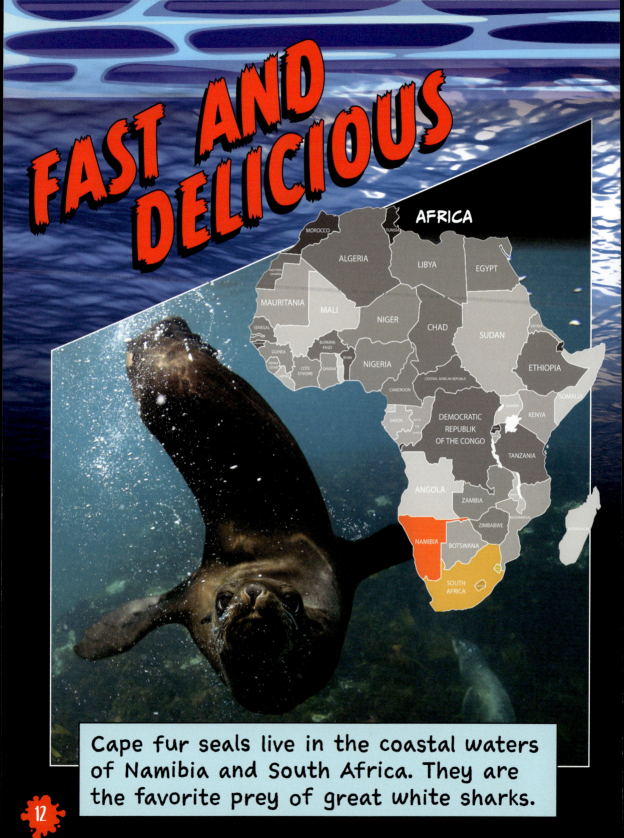

FAST AND DELICIOUS

Cape fur seals live in the coastal waters of Namibia and South Africa. They are the favorite prey of great white sharks.

GREAT WHITE SHARK

CAPE FUR SEAL

AFRICAN PENGUIN

Many ocean animals have the same **torpedo** shape. They glide through the water, using very little energy.

THE SEALS HAVE SHARP TEETH TO HOLD SLIPPERY FISH.

THE WATER IS COLD. TWO LAYERS OF FUR PROTECT THE SEALS. BLUBBER UNDER THEIR SKIN ADDS WARMTH.

GET OUT ALIVE!

A shark has three **blind spots**. It cannot see in front of its nose. It also sees nothing on each side of its body near the dorsal fin.

BLIND SPOT

BLIND SPOT

BLIND SPOT

A great white shark silently **stalks** the waters around a seal colony. It searches for its favorite meal. Target detected!

The shark shoots upward. It aims for the group of seals.

The great white breaches. A seal leaps away from the deadly jaws.

The seal leaps again and again.

Find Out More

Books

Murray, Julie. *Great White Shark*, Minneapolis, MN: Abdo Publishing, 2021

Pettiford, Rebecca. *Seals*, Minnetonka, MN: Bellwether Media, 2017

Websites

Search these online sources with an adult:

Cape Fur Seals | Animal Fact Guide

Great White Sharks | National Geographic Kids

Glossary

apex predators (AY-peks PRED-uh-turz) the top predator in an ecosystem

blind spots (BLAHYND SPOTS) hidden spaces around something, where the view is blocked

breach (BREECH) to launch up from the water's surface

coastal (KOH-stuhl) near the shore

colony (KAHL-uh-nee) a group of one kind of animal that lives together

constant (KON-stuhnt) without stopping

dorsal (DOR-suhl) located on an animal's back

ecosystems (EE-koh-sis-tumz) networks of plants and animals and how they interact with their environment and each other to survive

external (ek-STUR-nuhl) on the outside of something

prey (PRAY) animals hunted and eaten by other animals

stalks (STAWKS) hunts in a secretive way

torpedo (tor-PEE-doh) an underwater missile with a pointed nose and long, sleek shape

Index

blind spot(s) 18, 23
breach(es) 11, 22
dive(s) 14, 23
dorsal fin 9, 18

ecosystems 8
eyes 6
fish 7, 14, 16
prey 6, 10, 11, 12

pups 7, 13
swim(s) 9, 13, 19, 23
teeth 9, 16